Milly's Story

A Story of One Girl's Faith, Courage, Strength, and Survival

THERESA FRAZIER PALIK

ISBN 979-8-88616-758-0 (paperback)
ISBN 979-8-88943-151-0 (hardcover)
ISBN 979-8-88616-759-7 (digital)

Christian Faith Publishing
832 Park Avenue
Meadville, PA 16335
www.christianfaithpublishing.com

Cover art by Christiana Frazier

Printed in the United States of America

How could kindness almost cost someone their life?

I am a close friend of a girl named Milly. She has asked me if I would have the honor to tell her story. It is a story of courage, strength, survival, and faith. How could one person's act of kindness almost cost them their life? Please take this journey with me as I share Milly's story.

Milly was a small-town country girl. The kind of girl who could light up a room with her smile. She had big blue eyes and long auburn hair. You could always catch her in her favorite blue-and-white checkered dress that her mom had made for her, the one that was missing the top button. It's the one she hadn't gotten around to fixing with a stain from her dad's barbecue chicken that wouldn't come out. She felt most comfortable in bare feet. She loved feeling the cool earth and the light dew on the grass through her toes. She had the biggest heart of anyone around. She wanted to be everyone's best friend and would give the shirt off her back for another. She was always taught to treat others as you would like to be treated.

Always be kind and respectful. Her childhood was a good one. Memories of eating watermelon on a hot summer's night, picking strawberries with her mom, making mud pies, running through puddles, and building snow forts with her siblings.

She loved watching her dad play baseball and umpiring. Milly even kept score a few times. There were always a few furry creatures around the farm. Milly had her favorite cats, Princess and Black night, and her dog, Ladybird. Oh, yeah, and Freckles too. Milly had no worries except what hay bale she would lay on so she could daydream of the places in the world she longed to visit someday. Her chores would have to wait. She wanted to make sure the bluebirds would be in a sing-along to the tunes of "Amazing Grace."

She knew someday her prince charming would come and whisk her off to the beautiful "City of Light," Paris. Milly had longed to visit this most romantic city in France that she had read about in Mr. Smith's history class. The allure and charm of Paris were so delightful and exciting to this country girl. She longed to see the latest fashions of Valentino, Dior, and Chanel to name a few. To walk down the Champs-Élysées and visit the Arc de Triomphe and, of course, the symbol of love, the Eiffel Tower.

But for now, she would have to settle for the rolling fields of corn and strawberries on her farm, which was her world. Under an old oak tree, you would mostly find Milly curled up with her favorite book and a cool glass of sweet tea. She could smell the freshly cut grass as her dad had just finished mowing. There was going to be a cookout, so everything had to be neat and clean. Company was coming. Her mom was putting out the best tablecloths and making her famous deviled eggs and potato salad.

Today her friend, Earl, stopped by. A farm boy who knew his way around a tractor and horses. Earl always smelled of dust and dirt, but that is the cologne of a farm boy which was just fine with Milly. He was never without his yellow-brown straw hat that bore the years of sweat working on his dad's farm. Milly always said, "I'm going to buy you a new hat!"

Earl always replied, "This one is fine, Milly. I've had it for so long. It is shaped now to my head."

Earl had curly brown hair that peaked out from under his hat. He had hazel eyes and a crooked smile that always got Milly in a good mood. Earl and Milly were friends since they were knee-high to a grasshopper; two peas in a pod they would say. Where there was one, the other was. Earl had this old red Ford pickup truck that had seen better days but was perfect for Milly and Earl. The old farm truck had a lot of stories to tell for sure. The dent in the bumper where Earl was attempting to teach Milly to drive, and she backed up into Ms. Persis's old and green station wagon. Earl never fixed it, but they made it right with Ms. Persis by doing chores for her one summer around her farm.

Ms. Persis lived alone after her husband, John, passed away. She had a kind soul, rough around the edges, but she could cook the best peach cobbler within four counties. It was the kind of cobbler you could smell for miles and had just the right amount of crisp, crumble crust, and gooey peach filling. Of course, it was topped with a scoop of vanilla ice cream. She used the fresh peaches that were harvested the year before and were put up for the following year. Her peaches were the juiciest and most delicious around. Earl and Milly joked that Ms. Persis was the Julia Childs of the South.

They shared memories in that old pickup truck. Many Sunday afternoons, after church, they would end up at the lake by Milly's Grandma Winnie and Papa Stoney. They had permission to use one of the Jon boats and fish to their hearts' content. Earl was always the lucky one until one day Milly got her first fish. You would have thought she placed first in the State Fair! She was so excited that she dropped the fish, and away he swam in a zigzag line toward safety under a lily pad.

Milly wanted to keep their friendship and never wanted it to end. Days of running through the cornfields, watching the wild turkeys, the smell of sweet strawberries, and a light gentle breeze through her long red hair. Life was good. *How could things ever get better?* Milly thought. This was her world. A world filled with the laughter of her sisters and brothers chasing one another through the woods or catching a glimpse of the large green tractor that they had to see. Earl riding his horse to show off the new tricks he learned and her grandparents living across the woods. Mom and Dad always loving and hard working to provide a good life for the children.

Milly always had the comfort of family. She learned to appreciate southern cooking. The smells of her grandmother cooking some greens or her chocolate cake. Or her mom making an apple pie. Milly always liked to lick the bowl or just get a small taste. Sometimes sharing a sip from her dad's beer after he mowed the grass. She couldn't understand why it was so great, yuck! Sweet tea tasted much better to Milly.

Saturdays were for chores but started off with her mom cooking pancakes. Her pancakes, or shall we say flapjacks, were stacked high, fluffy, and would melt in your mouth. The butter and maple syrup melted over them with such ease. It was then off to hang laundry to dry on the clothesline. Milly would want to run through the freshly washed clothes that smelled so fragrant like a gentle breeze from the ocean. She would usually get a talking to from her mom, but that was Milly. Good-hearted Milly, always a dreamer.

She would say, "Mom, someday I want to be somebody. I want to travel and see places I've read about. I want to help people. Maybe I could be a nurse?"

Mom would always reply, "Sweet, little nipper, Milly, I love you. I think you should continue to learn from me and your grandmother on life on the farm and prepare to marry Earl someday!"

"Mom!" Milly shouted. "No, no, Earl is my friend, and besides, I'm going to marry my prince charming someday. He will whisk me out of my castle, and we will live happily ever after. Maybe I could be a mom someday like you and grandma?"

Well, for now, it was off to the chores of a farm girl. Tending to the cows, old Fanny was Milly's favorite. She was front and center and ready for a scratch. She was the leader of the cows. Then off to the chicken coop. Promptly there was Roscoe, the rooster, and his sidekick, Ethel the hen, to greet Milly. Milly would say, "What trouble have you been into?" Then she saw the plentiful eggs. Milly thought to herself, *Mom and Dad will be so excited. We will have eggs tomorrow for breakfast.*

Her dad always cooked eggs and toast on Sundays for the kids. Sunday also meant church day with grandma, her all-day meeting. Milly and her sister Carol went to church that day. Since Papa Ollie had passed away a few years back from a stroke, they went to give her company. Papa Ollie was a very gentle man. Milly has fond memories of him, and he would always say with a Ritz cracker in his hand, "Mm-hmm, good cracker." He smoked a pipe and worked hard on other neighboring farms. Grandma missed him a lot.

At the church that day, Carol and Milly were overcome with amusement by the fire and brimstone of the preacher. He was sweating something fierce. A large pitcher of water kept shaking every time he would beat his fists on the podium. It was quite a sight. Milly and Carol were trying to hold in their laughter, but the shaking bench gave way to their giggling. Their grandma was quick to keep them in line. It was nice being with her. She looked beautiful in her navy-and-white polka dot dress. She was very proper and classy, but grandma had a side of her only Milly and her siblings knew of. See she would every now and then get into some snuff and wild turkey. She would say, "Now, kids, don't tell on me."

The kids would always reply, "Grandma, we would never tell on you. Your secret is safe with us."

Milly had another grandma at the lake. Grandma Anne. She was very soft-spoken and the sweetest woman you would ever meet. She was beautiful but very strong and good-hearted. She always gave the best hugs. Here, Milly, her sister Carol, brother Adam, and sister Maria would all play for hours around the lake, chasing frogs and admiring the lily pads. The smell of fish wasn't too appealing, but their reward was helping their grandma in the snack and tackle shop.

Their Papa Oakley was working with their mom and dad and aunts and uncles to finish the log cabin up the hill. Papa Oakley was never seen without his cigar. Milly could smell his cigar as soon as he would light it up. The aroma of vanilla with a touch of cedar—that was Papa Oakley. They were all excited to see the cabin completed. Everyone was excited to share the holidays there together. It was a beautiful and magical place. After a long day at the lake, the evening sky was so clear. Milly found herself on the porch, listening to the frogs conversing back and forth. A whip-poor-will started his nightly calls to his mate. Life on the farm in Milly's world was perfect.

As time passed on the farm, it was time for the first high school graduation celebration. Milly and Earl were so excited about their big day. Seniors! Wow, they thought this day would never come. They were thinking of all the things they were going to do. The adventures they would go on. Saying goodbye to farm life, they would say. There is a big world out there just waiting for them. Milly's family had a country-style celebration, and they spared no expense. They had the finest fried chicken in the town, complete with potato salad, coleslaw, cornbread, their grandmother's chocolate cake, Mom's apple pie, and bluegrass music. Amidst all the festivities, her grandmother in the woods took her aside. She told her how proud she was of her.

"Milly, you go on and light up the world." But she said, "Be careful. Not everyone is going to see the beauty in you we see. Do not let anyone snuff out your light or break your spirit. Hold tight to the values you have learned from us and your farm life. Remember your angels are always with you, and the Lord above will guide you. Remember if you do come across trouble, you fight. Do whatever it takes to get away. Remember, I love you, and I'm always here for you."

Milly said she loved her too and that she was fine. "You worry too much, Grandma. I'm all grown-up now."

Her grandma gave her a big hug. "Remember where you come from and use that strength whenever you need to."

Her Mom and Dad told her how proud they were of her. They said to her, "You can do anything you set your mind to. You can achieve. Remember, family is everything and the Good Lord. You do not have to ever take a back seat to anyone. You are the apple of our eye, our 'little nipper.' We love you, and go out there and show the world who Milly is!"

Little did she know that soon, her life would be changed forever with one act of kindness. She would be facing a darkness that she never knew existed. It would put her in the fight of her life and far away from the safe and happy country life she grew up in.

Milly was awarded a scholarship to the business college, and Earl went to an out-of-state college to study soil science. Every school break, Earl would come back and meet up with Milly. They would join other friends at the local pizza hangout. The pizza was the best around. On any given morning, you could smell the aromas coming from the brick oven. Everyone in town wanted to know what the latest creation by Joe was.

Joe was from Italy. His pizza was a true treat; it was the cheesiest and had the crispiest crust and the best homemade sauce on the planet. The town became known because of his pizza and would come from miles to partake. The best was pepperoni, sausage, and mushrooms according to Milly, but Earl liked pineapple and ham and sometimes all of the works. You could smell the aroma from the brick oven down the street from Uncle Randy's and Aunt Catherine's house.

One Saturday evening, the gang all got together at their favorite hangout. It was like old times, seeing friends you hadn't seen in a while. Milly was feeling extra pretty that night. She had just had her hair colored by Susan and wearing her new boots, blue jeans, a heart necklace Earl gave her for her birthday, and her favorite white lace top. *This was going to be a great night*, she thought. They were going to play some pool, try the new draft beer on tap, and order the special pizza Joe had prepared.

It was a large group of them since it was the summer break. Most of the usual friends were there and a few new ones. There was this one guy that stood out. He had a bright red shirt on, new Levi's jeans, and cowboy boots. He had been around the group a few times, but this was the first time Earl had met him. Earl right away did not have a good feeling about him. He mentioned this to Milly. He said, "Milly, we've known each other since elementary school, you trust me, right?"

Milly said, "Of course."

"Well, this new guy in the group. I get a bad feeling about him."

Milly said, "Why? He seems fine. He's a painter and studying to go abroad. He's in the local rodeo the next city over. He just bought us all a round of beers. He's hung out with us a few times and seems nice. I believe he has a girlfriend and a young baby but comes to the pizza place to get a break."

Earl still did not have a good feeling but was willing to give him a big country welcome to the group. It was a great night of reminiscing, line dancing, and enjoying life with their old group. After several rounds of pool, beers, wings, and five pizzas later, it was getting late. Earl was the designated driver for others who had a little too much. Milly only had one beer and didn't even finish that. She loves cream soda, and Joe had the best on tap.

Earl said to Milly, "I'm going to call it a night." Earl had to get up early the next morning to work in his dad's fields for the summer break.

Milly said, "Okay, I'll call you tomorrow. Maybe we can go down to the lake and do some fishing?"

Earl said, "Sounds good but call me when you get home."

Milly said, "You worry too much, Earl. I'm fine. I'm here with our friends and just one more round of pool, and I must try some of Joe's new dessert, the tower of chocolate."

Earl said, "Okay, but not too late."

Milly said, "Okay, Dad, LOL."

Earl gave Milly a big hug and said goodbye to everyone and headed off in his old red pickup truck. The group started to break up, but the new guy was still there. Milly had struck up a conversation about the rodeo and the arts. She always loved to paint and wanted someday to go to Paris. The new guy said he was going to Paris. Milly thought this was incredible. They also shared the same taste in movies.

She asked, "Do you need a ride?"

He answered, "I just live around the corner and had walked to the pizza place."

Milly, being the good-hearted country girl, said, "Nonsense, I can give you a ride. It's not that far, and we may get a rain shower tonight."

Milly drove off in her cobalt-blue convertible Camaro with the new guy. It was a nice summer night, so Milly had put the top down. The stars were out, and the latest country song was playing on her stereo. While driving to drop off the new guy, Earl called Milly.

"Milly, are you home yet? I hadn't heard from you and wanted to make sure you were okay. I was worried about you."

Milly answered, "I'm fine. I'm just dropping off the new guy and will be home shortly. I'll call you back in a few minutes."

Earl replied, "Milly, I'm afraid for you. I heard some things about him. Please drop him off soonest and call me. I'll come to where you are, just tell me."

Milly answered, "Don't be silly, Earl. I'm fine. We'll go fishing tomorrow. It's supposed to be great weather. I'll talk to you later." Milly hung up. Milly was then asking the new guy, "So which house is yours? I am not familiar with this street."

It was quite dark, and the moon was just starting to peek out of the clouds. A light breeze started to come up. An owl started screeching, and Milly heard the calls of the frogs from the nearby pond, much like at the farm. New construction had just started on this section of town. Some folks had moved in but were not expected until a few weeks later. The streetlights were not all hooked up yet. She could hear a dog barking in the distance. Milly noticed a sign that said, "Dead end." Milly then asked, "Which is your house? It's getting late, and I have to get home."

There wasn't an answer from the new guy. It was then that Milly started to become nervous. She thought to herself, *What have I done? Who is this guy? Was Earl, right?* Milly tried again to get an answer out of him—nothing. This time, Milly put her car in park, headlights still on, stereo on, and asked again, "Which is your house?" It was then that things took a turn for the worse.

He replied, "I need you to do this for me."

Milly replied, "Do what?"

He then put his hand on top of Milly's and brandished a box cutter. He said, "Turn off the car's headlights and do as I say, or I will cut your throat."

It was then that the new guy became her attacker and kidnapper. He became another person. He was so dark and cold. She felt that she was looking at the face of someone who had so much anger and was going to hurt her. Milly couldn't believe what was happening. She kept thinking, *If I can talk to him, reason with him, then maybe he would stop this.* Milly pleaded with him, "Please, stop! I'll take you wherever you want. Let's talk about the rodeo, Paris, and painting."

He didn't want to. He then said, "Do this for me, or I'll kill you. I'm going to cut your throat."

Milly said, "Please, no. Please. I need to get home to my family. They are waiting for me, please."

He then said, "Well, you do not like me like Earl."

She said, "That's not true. Earl and I have been friends since we were little. Please, we can work this out." For a moment, there was a pause. Milly was then able to hit the horn on her car. He then attacked her with the box cutter. Milly was fighting with him in her car. She then was able to run, but every time she would get away, he caught up to her. It seemed like he had superhuman strength. He then slammed her into the open car door. She gasped out loud in pain and kept screaming for help. She tried again to get back into her car and succeeded, but he then dragged her out. She was punching, scratching, anything she could, yelling, "Help me! Someone, help me!"

She kept thinking, *I must either drive off without him in the car or get to one of the houses on the street for help*. Milly only saw one house in the far distance with a porch light on. Her plan was to leave in her car or get to that house—do whatever it took to survive this. She thought to herself, *How could I let this happen? Why is he doing this to me? I should have listened to Earl.*

Her phone had fallen underneath the seat somewhere in the struggle. She couldn't reach it and call for help. At this point, she was fighting with him and being cut with the box cutter as she struggled to get it from him. Milly was cut badly in the process. Her favorite white top was now covered in blood. She had been cut bad on her hand, and now he had the box cutter to her throat.

He said, "Get out of the car and do as I say, or I will cut your throat."

Fearing for her life, she complied. She tried to get space between the box cutter and her throat. Her thought was if she created space and her hand was cut, then her throat would be spared. Her hand was cut more and now bleeding uncontrollably. It was then that she was dragged from her car to the side of the road, in a cul-de-sac. Milly could smell the freshly cut grass, and it started to sprinkle a little. She was then tied up with her jeans over her head. She was naked now from the waist down, no shoes, bloodied, fingernails missing, and her necklace torn from her. She was bruised and battered. She looked ripped to shreds by this monster.

Milly feared what would come next. *I will put myself in another place*, she thought. I will be back on the farm in the cornfields and smelling strawberries. Milly thought if he gets what he wants, he will let her go. *I'll survive this.* Milly was violently sexually assaulted. For what seemed like an eternity of horror, she thought, *Okay, he will leave. He got what he wanted.* After this savage attack and violation of her body, she struggled to gain enough strength to stand. She realized that she was naked from the waist down and bleeding immensely from her injuries. Her beautiful new white top was now a bright shade of red. The necklace Earl gave her was nowhere to be found. Her red hair was matted and stained by her blood. She couldn't find her shoes, and it was hard to see. She felt this overwhelming amount of pain rush over her whole body. It was like she had been in the fight of her life. Milly thought this was her chance to run. She attempted to run, but her knees were badly injured, and she could barely stand. Her shoes were missing, but she mustered up enough strength to run.

It was then that he grabbed her by her arm and threw her on her back and started choking her with his bare hands. Milly looked up at the clear sky with the stars shining down and said to herself, *This is the night I am going to die.* She saw Earl and her family and friends flash before her eyes. She remembered having an out-of-body experience, floating over her body and seeing what was being done to her. It was quiet, calm, and warm; and she saw a light. It was then that suddenly she was back down in her body. She was looking into the cold eyes of her attacker. It was much like a shark's expression before they attack their prey. Milly said the expression of hate on his face was something she would never forget.

Milly asked herself, *How could another human being do this to another?* He was a monster. A monster she knew would have to fight if she wanted to remain alive. She felt things start to get dark and close in on her as he proceeded to choke her. She was able to get her hands between his and her neck. She gasped a few breaths. She then remembered a few things from her introduction to jujitsu such as the strongest part of a woman is her legs. You are not going to be able to overpower a man more than likely. She was able to push him off her.

She ran on the dark pavement on her bare feet, her skin tearing, and cuts were forming on the bottoms of her feet, legs, and knees as she was being knocked down and tripped. She was naked from the waist down, bloodied, and weak. She was losing a lot of blood from her wounds. She kept yelling, "Help! Help!" Her voice was so weak that she thought no one would hear her, but she kept screaming as loud as she could. She continued to run toward the one house on the cul-de-sac that had a porch light on. It seemed like a beacon of hope to Milly in this darkness. A guiding light that would show her the way to survival and safety. She was so close to the porch. She thought to herself, *I'm going to survive this. I've made it.* But her attacker caught up to her.

He dragged her back by her hair with such force she could feel her hair pulling out of her scalp. He was pulling with all his might and said, "Get in the trunk. You are going to be my hostage for the night. I'm going to do what I want to you."

Milly yelled, "No! I will not!"

He proceeded to hit her with a flurry of punches with his fists to her head, body, and back and knocked her down. He kept pulling her hair.

Milly yelled, "You will have to pull my hair out! I'm not going with you!" She remembered what her grandmother had said, *Fight with all your might! Do not go to another location with them. You remember the strength you learned from your family. Survive at all costs.* Milly kept fighting. She became angry that this person had done this to her. She was going to fight like hell. He then threw her into a brick flower planter. Milly yelled out in pain but got back up and continued toward the porch with the light on.

They were now fighting on the lawn of the house, and she kept being dragged back toward her car. She was exhausted and losing ground. She was in a lot of pain. It was then that he grabbed her again, pulling her hair. He then knocked her down and kicked her in the jaw. Milly collapsed but got back up again and ran as fast as she could to the porch with the light on. Then a man and a woman appeared and yelled out, "Hey, what are you doing?" The guy then ran and jumped into Milly's car and drove off with her purse and cell phone. The couple took Milly in. They gave her clothes and called 911.

Milly was safe. They were Milly's angels who had just moved in a week earlier to their new home. The husband said he heard something outside and went to see what it was. With all the air conditioners running, it was divine intervention that he was able to hear Milly's cries for help. Milly's car was found abandoned by a pond. The police said her attacker intended to put Milly in the trunk of her car and push it into the pond. He was arrested two days later at his apartment where he lived with his girlfriend and baby. He had the clothes he was wearing the night of her assault. There was so much physical evidence it was not hard. He confessed and spent a year in jail until the day in court. With all of the continuations and stalling by the defense, it seemed like Milly would never get closure so she could move on her with her life and heal.

Milly could not walk for two weeks. She had two black eyes; bruises covered most of her body. She had multiple stitches on her hands, feet, and head. Her tooth was broken, and her back was so bruised and scraped up from landing repeatedly on the pavement over and over again. Her knees were so badly injured that in order to clean the wounds out, they had to give her morphine.

At the hospital, she didn't want her parents, siblings, or Earl to see her like this. She asked if they could clean her up before they saw her. Her family had to bathe her and help her get around. She was in so much pain. She couldn't or wanted to drive a car for quite some time. It was hard, Milly said, to look at herself in the mirror. Even after the bruises started going away and she was healing, she still saw the beaten and bruised self of a farm girl she once knew. She is self-conscious to wear shorts due to the scars on her knees from the attack. Someone so full of life and never thought an act of kindness would be turned against her by such a dark, poor excuse of a human being. She had to wait a year for her day in court. She was supported by a member of the Special Victims Unit.

Milly learned the attack was approximately over two hours. It seemed like an eternity for Milly. She realized that her life would be on display for the whole world to see. Her character was put in question. The defense did their job but seemed to grasp at anything to get their client off and to go as far as create lies and was not going to allow her pictures of her injuries to be immiscible in court as it would sway the jury.

Thank the dear Lord that her pictures were allowed because the judge felt the jury needed to see the results of the violent attack on Milly. She was told, "Please hang in there. It is going to be one of the hardest things you do, and you will have to relive this terrifying event all over again at the trial." If she did not testify, he would probably walk. Milly did not want him to get away with this. She did not want him to be able to hurt another person ever again. Milly was so scared to be in the same room with the person who tried to kill her. It was so hard to say what happened to a room full of strangers and your family and friends. You are victimized all over again by the defense attorneys.

Milly's anxiety was very high. Her hands would start to tremble. She would become nauseous. She would listen to country music to calm her nerves before she had to testify. Milly was very brave. She showed courage and strength she never knew she had. She was able to testify, and Milly's attacker was found guilty on all charges; each was a felony. Then sentencing came. Her family had written victim impact statements as to why her attacker should be shown no mercy since Milly wasn't shown any mercy.

She begged him to stop, and he didn't. As her family read their impact statements, holding hands, fighting back tears, one by one, they each looked at Milly's attacker. He had no remorse and had such cold, lifeless eyes. The family was able to say their piece and implore the court that he deserved the maximum each charge carried. They did not want him to be able to hurt another person like he had hurt their beautiful Milly. They did not want another family to go through the pain that they had for the last year. They showed such courage and fortitude. His crimes had escalated. He was put away for the rest of his life with no chance of parole.

The most liberating and pivotal point in the trial was when Milly was allowed to give her victim impact statement. She was now able to take back control from the night he took away from her and say what she wanted to without fear. She looked this monster in the eyes and said, "Why? I only showed you kindness. You could have let me go. I begged for you to stop. Everyone has a choice, and you chose to hurt me. My angels are with me in this courtroom today as they were with me the night of my assault. You tried to extinguish my light, but you were not successful. I am going to walk out of this courtroom today and go on with my life, you are not. You will spend the rest of your days in prison."

Milly thanked her dear Lord, her family and friends, and the court. This part is so important for victims and their families. You will never get a chance again, and you don't want to have regrets. Milly's attacker was given the maximum sentence on each felony charge. He will spend the rest of his life in prison.

With the help of a relentless, determined Irish detective and good police work, they caught him. He never gave up on Milly's case and was there with her every step of the way. Milly called him her "knight in shining armor." Also, she wanted to thank the brave woman who had filed a report a few years earlier of a man who tried to attack her and had similar features and the same description. If it were not for her and the determination and some divine intervention from Milly's angels, she would not be here today.

Milly, for the longest time, was very ashamed of the *accident*, she would call it. It was hard to put into words her *assault*. She did not think she was strong or worthy of ever getting back to the once-so-free, happy farm girl who loved life and only wanted to help others. I am proud to say that she is that same girl. It has changed her, of course, but she did not let this monster take more away from her than he did that night. She now has the power over him.

I feel very honored to call Milly my friend, and she entrusted me to share her story. It took a very courageous and strong woman to survive what she did and live to tell her story. She is still only thinking of helping others. Milly is truly an angel living among us, and I feel very honored to have her in my life every day.

So many people reached out and sent flowers to Milly. In time, her physical wounds healed; but the emotional ones took a lot longer. Through her faith, her mother and father, her Earl, and her close-knit family and friends, therapy with her life coach, determination, courage, her dog Ladybird, and perseverance, she was able to piece her life back. She also speaks of her angels who were with her that fateful night. She believes they were the ones who gave her strength. Her beloved grandparents who had since passed on were there with her. She married the love of her life, Earl. She has traveled the world with Earl. They did make it to Paris. Nature was a passion Earl and Milly shared together. They have been to quite a few of the National Parks. The Caribbean is their favorite place.

Earl is her hero who saved her from her castle and moat. Her love of her life was always there; she just had to look. Her heart necklace was returned to her from that night. Earl had it repaired, and Milly never takes it off. She went on to have a successful career in business, a beautiful home, a new furry child, children, and grandchildren, lots of nieces and nephews, and great friends. She thanks God every day she was given a second chance at life and never wants to take a single sunrise or sunset, the laughter of a child, snow falling, birds chirping, or the joy of life for granted.

She says, "Buy that pair of shoes, run through the grass barefoot, take that trip, go to that concert, tell someone you love them, give hugs, praise God, eat that cake, love yourself, and be kind to others that are worthy."

Milly wanted to share her story to bring awareness and be relatable to anyone who had gone through this type of trauma or was a victim or family member of a violent attack. Milly would say she is a survivor. She says this did happen to her, but it does not define her. She has her good and bad days. She felt broken and was afraid to be Milly. She was always a kind, generous, trusting, loving life, beautiful, spirited person. She thought being who she was had got her in trouble, and her kindness almost cost her, her life. In time, she learned that her attacker chose to do this. She is not as trusting and has her guard up.

Her message is this: Listen to your instincts, your friends. Always stay in groups. You never know what someone is capable of. If you see someone in need of help, call 911 or a cab/Uber for them. There are predators out there waiting for their opening. They are the true darkness of humanity. Be vigilant and strong.

Milly said her kindness was used against her and that she went on with her life. Her attacker will spend the rest of his days thinking about what he did to a kind and beautiful person. Milly rebuilt her life, got married to Earl, and has children, grandchildren, and furry children. She says the scars are there, and she thought no one would ever love her or accept her. She thought she was damaged and ashamed, but with the love of her life, Earl, her angels, her family, and friends, most importantly the good Lord, and her sheer willingness to fight, she was able to overcome the darkest night of her life.

Her early years of childhood, she said, helped her through the darkest hour of her life and her faith. She said she always will remember where she came from and is forever grateful to her parents and grandparents for the morals and beliefs they instilled in her. She gives so much gratitude for the love and support of her siblings, all her other family members, and friends.

She says, "I'm beautiful, and no one will ever take my spirit away. I'm a strong country girl! Farm life is where I come from!"

Milly dedicates this story to the love of her life, Earl, her family, friends, her Lord, the angels, the police detectives, fire and rescue, the couple who rescued her, the SVU unit, the court, and her community for making sure this monster never saw the light of day again. Milly wants to send a message that there are consequences to your actions. Also, to all her beautiful sisters out there and their families who can relate to her story. You are so brave and strong. Never forget how beautiful you are and do not doubt your worth.

Milly understands that unfortunately, not every-one's story ends like hers. She knows far too many women who have fallen to these predators; they are the pure darkness of humanity with no regard for life. She prays and sends her love and support to the families where their loved ones are not here today but are angels watching over them.

Milly wanted to send this message: Always remember, you are stronger than you think. If you find yourself in a situation like this, you fight or flight, never give up, run for help, scream, punch, kick, and learn to listen and trust your instincts. Be safe, my beautiful women. You are gorgeous on the inside and outside no matter what you have been through. You are worthy and deserving of the good things in life. Do not let a traumatic experience or a setback keep you from your destiny.

Milly told me that she always wondered why she was saved. What purpose did she have? Why did God save her? I told Milly, "I believe I know. You did it when you survived your attack and put this monster away so he couldn't hurt anyone else ever again." I truly believe her story needs to be told, and if it helps just one person, then she has fulfilled her destiny; this is why she was saved.

Much love,
Storyteller, a good friend of Milly's
(Based on a true story)

About the Author

Theresa Frazier Palik was born in a small town in Virginia. She loves to travel. She lives in Virginia with the love of her life and her furry child, Bella, a yellow Labrador. She loves animals and nature. She feels most free either at the beach or in nature somewhere. Family and the Lord are the most important things in her life. Her angels and her friends too are a big part of her life. She loves to dance, do aerobics, and paint. She is a big sports fan and loves to attend baseball games. She loves beautiful colors and fashion. She loves and lives life to the fullest. She always says, "Buy that pair of shoes, eat that piece of cake, take that trip, tell someone you love them, and give them a hug." She is also a big Kenny Chesney fan. She loves country music or anything that has a good beat to it.